cloverleaf books™

Community Helpers

Let's Meet a Librarian

Gina Bellisario

illustrated by **Ed Myer**

M MILLBROOK PRESS · MINNEAPOLIS

For my children's book helpers —G.B.

To my nephew George —E.M.

The publisher wishes to thank Roberta Boegel, Collection
Development Librarian, Sacramento Public Library, and Chelsea
Couillard, Youth Materials Selector, Sacramento Public Library,
for sharing their knowledge, expertise, and advice.

Millbrook Press
A division of Lerner Publishing Group, Inc.
241 First Avenue North
Minneapolis, MN 55401 USA

For reading levels and more information, look up this title at
www.lernerbooks.com.

Main body text set in Slappy Inline 18/28.
Typeface provided by T26.

Library of Congress Cataloging-in-Publication Data

Bellisario, Gina.
   Let's meet a librarian / by Gina Bellisario ; illustrated by Ed
Myer.
      pages   cm. — (Cloverleaf books. Community helpers)
   Includes index.
   ISBN 978-0-7613-9027-5 (lib. bdg.)
   ISBN 978-1-4677-1047-3 (EB pdf)
   1. Librarians—Juvenile literature. 2. Libraries—Juvenile
literature. I. Myer, Ed, illustrator. II. Title.
Z682.B45 2013
020.92—dc23   2012022460

Manufactured in the United States of America
3 - 41536 - 12580 - 9/30/2016

TABLE OF CONTENTS

Chapter One

The Spy

Our class is on a mission. We're going to find out what a **librarian** does. We decide to visit Mr. Field. He's our school librarian.

MR. FIELD

Librarians are people in the community. A community is a group of people who live in the same city, town, or neighborhood.

"I'm an **information expert**," says Mr. Field.

"What does that mean?" asks Joey.

"Let me show you," he says. "What's something you really like?"

"Dinosaurs!" says Joey.

Mr. Field uses his computer to track down a *T. rex.* Then he tells Joey how to find books in the library about the *T. rex.*

Search: T. Rex

1. T. Rex Up Close
2. Incredible Dinos: T. Rex
3. How to Draw a T. Rex
4. T. Rex and Other Dinosaurs

"How did you do that?" asks Joey. Mr. Field says we can look for books about *anything* using the **online catalog.**

A librarian named Melvil Dewey made finding books easy. He gave different numbers to different types of books. Librarians use the numbers to put the books in order. Many libraries use these numbers.

The catalog is Mr. Field's **librarian tool**. It lists all the books and movies in our library. He can also see things in other libraries.

CATALOG

KIDS | TEENS

SEARCH
• Title o Author o Subject

o Keyword

Library books don't have to stay in the library. Students and teachers can check out books from the school library. Librarians use computers to keep track of what books are checked out. So return your books on time!

Maybe Mr. Field is a spy.

Chapter Two

No Shushing Allowed!

Uh-oh. Jack is **talking** in the library.

"SHH!" whispers Grace.

PLAY AREA

But Mr. Field doesn't mind. He says making noise can help us learn. He plays music from around the world. Mr. Field can get *loud!*

Most people study best in a quiet library. So many libraries have separate places for noisy learning. These are called play areas or story rooms.

Speaking up is important for librarians.
It is how they share information.

Sometimes, librarians invite guests to speak at the library. The guest might be a nurse, a dog trainer, or a magician. Librarians call on them for extra information.

They give library tours and puppet shows.

Librarians are **full of facts**. Reading so much helps them know about all kinds of things.

Librarians like hearing from you too. So ask a librarian a question, and pump up your brainpower!

Chapter Three

A ComputerWizard

Our teacher Mrs. Ríos needs help.
Her computer is stuck.

Presto! Mr. Field came to the rescue. He says librarians are **technology wizards.**

Many libraries have electronic books, also called e-books. You use a computer or other electronic reader to look at an e-book. Librarians can show you how they work. Librarians learn about new technology.

Mr. Field is good at **troubleshooting.**
Troubleshoot means "to solve problems."

VIRUS
FREE

AREA

Sometimes computers can get viruses. A virus stops a computer from working properly. Librarians use special technology to help keep computers safe from viruses.

He teaches us how to use computers to do our school work. And he teaches our teacher how to keep our computers safe from viruses.

Mrs. Ríos can save the day!

Not every librarian lends a hand in school. Some help out in museums or in hospitals. Librarians also work at public libraries. These libraries are open to the community.

Mr. Field came to read us a story.
So we give our book helper a hand too!

Go on a Book Hunt

Most libraries have books on many different topics. A topic is what the book is about. A librarian can track down books on any topic you want. So can you. Would you like to read about butterflies? Or how about police cars? Use the library catalog and go on a book hunt.

What you need:
a computer, open to your library's catalog page
a piece of scrap paper
a pencil

1) Decide what your topic will be. Do you like books about trains? Horses? Type your topic into the library catalog page. You can find this page on a library computer or a home computer. Make sure your topic is spelled correctly. Press Enter and presto! You will see a list of book titles. Pick a title of a book that you want to look for. Write the title on the piece of paper.

2) Now you need the book's call number. A call number tells where a book is in the library. Most call numbers are made up of letters and numbers. Write the call number next to the title. This information will help you track down your book.

3) Going on a book hunt? Be sure to bring a grown-up too. Sometimes, books are hard to find. They might be in the wrong place or checked out. If the book you want isn't in the library, don't worry. There are tons more on the shelf!

GLOSSARY

catalog: a complete list of items, usually found on a computer, that can be borrowed from a library

community: a group of people who live in the same area

e-book: an electronic book

electronic reader: a tool with which a person can read an e-book

public library: a library that is open to anyone in a community

technology: the tools people make to improve life. Technology in libraries includes bar codes and computers.

troubleshoot: to solve problems

viruses: harmful programs that stop computers from working properly

BOOKS

Cleary, Brian. *Do You Know Dewey? Exploring the Dewey Decimal System.*
Minneapolis: Millbrook Press, 2013.
This picture book follows a group of adventurous kids exploring a library as they discover what is in each hundreds section of the Dewey decimal system.

Heos, Bridget. *Let's Meet a Teacher.* Minneapolis: Millbrook Press, 2013.
Find out more about another community helper who works inside our schools.

Houston, Gloria. *Miss Dorothy and Her Bookmobile.* New York: HarperCollins, 2011.
Read the story of a real librarian who made a library on wheels.

Murray, Julie. *Librarians.* Edina, MN: Abdo Publishing, 2011.
This book has photos that show what librarians do at work.

WEBSITES

Career Spotlight: Rare Book Conservator
http://www.kids.gov/video/conservator.shtml
This website has a movie about a librarian who fixes very old books.
The librarian works at the Library of Congress in Washington, D.C.

LERNER *e* **SOURCE**™
Expand learning beyond the printed book. Download free, complementary educational resources for this book from our website, www.lerneresource.com.

It's Never Too Soon . . . to Start Thinking about a Career as a Librarian
http://www.ala.org/ala/educationcareers/careers/librarycareerssite/children_flier.pdf
Visit the American Library Association website to see this fun flier about a librarian's job.

KidsClick!
http://www.kidsclick.org
This website from the School of Library and Information Science at Kent State University in Ohio was made by librarians for kids. You can search an online catalog and use the Dewey decimal system.